REtoday Services

Developing Primary

D1795094

Introduction

'Words of wisdom are a stream that flows from a deep mountain.'
Proverbs 18:4

All religions have sacred writings or oral traditions passed down through generations. These provide the basis for belief and doctrine, and provide believers with guidance for living. A key aspect of any programme of Religious Education is to introduce pupils to these sacred books and to enable them to explore their insights and influence both for believers and for others.

As teachers we spend time exploring with pupils what these sacred books mean for believers, how they are used in worship and how they are treated with respect as sources of authority and guidance. All of these matters are very important – but equally important is the need for pupils to move beyond the externals of religious practice and to engage with what these holy books actually say. Pupils need to be set activities which enable them to encounter these teachings and reflect for themselves on what makes them so deeply significant in the lives of millions of people today.

This publication aims to help you do just that. It suggests some practical activities which will challenge primary pupils not only to *learn about*, but also to *learn from* some of the teachings found in these sacred books and to reflect on what might be valuable sources of wisdom, guidance and inspiration for their own lives.

Joyce Mackley
Editor

Things to note...

Many of the activities in this book complement QCA RE scheme of work 6C: Why are sacred texts important?

Contents

Getting pupils talking and thinking

Four starter activities for introducing a topic on sacred texts as sources of wisdom and inspiration

Activity 1: Favourite sayings

→ Ask pupils to share any favourite sayings or good advice about living.

→ Share your own wise words with pupils. Talk about what they mean to you and where they came from.

→ Collect together words of guidance and wisdom for a wall display. These could be sayings, quotes, stories. Involve the whole school community by asking parents, teachers, midday supervisors, governors to share a wise saying or quote they love with you. You may already have some displayed on posters around the school. Some examples are given in the next activity.

> My favourite saying…
> 'Good, better, best, never let it rest, until the good is better and the better best.'
> I was taught this at primary school – it means you must always try your best at everything.
> *12-year-old*

Do the right thing even if it is hard.

Before you say what you think – think!

No matter what you say, it's what you do that speaks for you.

The best way to have a friend is to be one.

Life is full of choices – choose carefully.

What is popular is not always right; what is right is not always popular.

We learn little from success but much from failure. *(Arab saying)*

Activity 2: Some good advice? 'Say what you think' activity

This activity works well with younger primary pupils as well as older ones. It promotes speaking and listening skills and ensures everyone takes an active part.

→ Mark out three big circles on the floor with rope – one marked 'agree', one marked 'disagree', one marked 'not sure'.

→ Display statements of popular wisdom like those on the left, one at a time, on an overhead projector screen.

→ Explain to pupils that as each piece of advice is displayed they must think carefully about it for 30 seconds (60 seconds for older pupils), work out whether they agree or disagree with it, and work out one reason for their opinion, which they should be ready to share if asked. If they are not sure, they need to be able to explain why.

→ Pupils stand in the circles to represent their viewpoints. The teacher asks individuals from each circle to give their reasons. Other questions can be posed to stimulate more discussion. Take a class vote to decide the best 'Words of Wisdom' from those on offer.

→ Consider where such words of wisdom, guidance and inspiration might be found. Gather pupils' ideas and encourage them to link with earlier learning in RE.

AGREE

NOT SURE

DISAGREE

Activity 3: Ten tips for life

Many religions have lists of advice for living. Christianity and Judaism have the ten commandments, Buddhism has five precepts and eight steps to happiness (the noble eightfold path).

➜ As a starter activity, pupils could devise their own **10tips4life**. You may like to use the ideas suggested by Rosie (on the right) as a starting point.

10tips4life

Sing and dance as though no one can see and hear you

Speak from your heart and mind

Smile and people will smile with you

Stand up, be strong, be brave

Rosie, aged 9

Activity 4: Wise words

Pupils could:

➜ take a wise saying from a faith tradition (preferably expressed in pupil-friendly language) – see the examples alongside from Jesus.

➜ brainstorm ideas about what they think the wise saying means.

➜ work out a situation today where the wise saying might apply, and devise a mime or role-play to show this; take turns to act these out to the rest of the class, asking the other pupils to suggest what the wise saying might be.

➜ have a class vote: Is this particular saying good advice for today?

Some wise sayings from Jesus

These are pupil-friendly versions of things Jesus said:

Never try to get back at someone who makes you cry.

Worrying about what might happen is a waste of time.

If you fight you will get hurt by fighting.

You should love people you don't like and be good to those who are horrible to you.

Sources of these wise sayings

1 Matthew 5:39 (Jesus' teaching on revenge in the Sermon on the Mount)

2 Matthew 6:34 (Jesus' teaching on worry in the Sermon on Mount)

3 Matthew 26:52 (Arrest of Jesus in the garden of Gethsemane)

4 Luke 6:27 (Jesus' teaching on loving others)

Things to note

Religious sacred texts are often called 'Special Books'. This term provides a useful starting point but it is important to remember that teaching must get beyond this idea. These texts are regarded by believers as sacred, holy or inspired writing which commands obedience. They are not 'special' in the same sense as a pupil's favourite story book. Teaching needs to extend pupils' understanding by introducing the terminology of sacred writing carefully.

Sacred Texts in the national literacy strategy

The National Literacy Strategy classifies texts as either fiction or non-fiction. Fiction is defined as 'text which is invented by a writer or speaker'. Sacred texts often contain stories, but if they are placed in 'fiction' many people will be offended at the implication that their sacred texts are 'invented'. Sacred texts have a deep level of meaning for members of a faith community. RE must allow for the religious significance and meaning of the literary text to be explored.

Wisdom from the Bible

For the teacher

The Bible is well described as a source of wisdom for Christians. It is sometimes suggested that it is the most unread best-seller in the world, but actually, millions of Christians read the Bible daily, and millions base their spiritual life on its teaching and inspiration. When studying the Bible in class, at least five approaches could be taken:

- **Historical** study will investigate such questions as: what events do the Bible's writers record? What is the significance of these events?

- **Religious** study will investigate such questions as: what was the religion of the Bible in its own time? How has the religious influence of the Bible affected us today?

- **Theological** study will investigate such questions as: what do the Bible's writers believe about God, or humanity? Are their views true? How could we know?

- **Spiritual** study will investigate the question: do the Bible's writings inspire, motivate or challenge the spiritual and moral life of readers?

- **Learning from the Bible** will investigate the questions: does the Bible have wisdom to offer readers today? What are my own reflections on the 'wisdom of the Bible'?

In this section, seven activities for the classroom are suggested. The activities are intended to enable a focus on the Bible as a source of authority or guidance to those for whom it is a sacred writing, covering some learning needs for ages 5–11.

They include a trust game, a thinking skills strategy, a matching activity about metaphors for the Bible, a guided story for use with a stilling exercise, and a more extended and creative approach to the wisdom of the Bible which uses the music of Martyn Joseph. It is suggested that activities 1, 2 and 5 may be better suited to younger pupils, but all are flexible.

Activity 1: Words can guide us

Use a simple 'Blindfold walking game' to help pupils understand that words can guide us. Get one pupil to walk across the classroom blindfolded while another gives them directions. This is always popular and they'll all want a turn, so set up the activity in pairs after a demonstration. After taking turns to guide and to be guided, ask pupils to complete three sentences (in writing or by talking):

- If you can't see, then it's good to trust…
- If someone else trusts you to guide them, you should…
- We all need to be guided in life, for example…

Discuss their answers, and relate the activity to the ways in which sacred words, in Christianity the words of God in the Bible, can guide.

Activity 2: Favourite books

Ask pupils to talk at home about the books or stories that have been their favourites at different ages. Discuss ways in which our needs and loves in books change. The books we love give us some entertainment, some wisdom, something to think about. Link this to the reasons why the Bible is 'much loved' by Christians. It contains wise words, rulebooks, stories, histories, miracles, and ideas about how to live well. This leads in to Activity 3.

Activity 3: Exploring the popularity of the Bible – a thinking skills activity

The Bible is the world's best-selling book ever. The whole Bible has been translated into over 330 different languages, and the New Testament alone has been translated into a further 800+ languages.

In this simple thinking skills task, pupils in groups of two or three are asked to take the six explanations opposite for why the Bible is so popular, and make a six-slice pie chart – see template on page 6. The six slices on the 'pie' are to be of different sizes: the biggest slice for the best explanation, the smaller slices for ones the pupils judge less good, a mere sliver for the least satisfactory explanation. This can be simplified for young pupils, but 8-year-olds can do this simple judgement task through discussion.

Metacognition questions
(these kinds of question concentrate on *how the learners were thinking* as they tackled the task):

- What was easy and what was difficult about this task?
- What did you notice about the six ideas about the Bible you were given as you did this activity?
- What did you learn about the popularity of the Bible?
- Is it simple or complicated to explain?
- In what ways were your partners a help to you in thinking this issue through?
- How would you do this differently if you did it again?
- Did it help you to understand the range of points made when you saw them on the 'pie'? How does this work?
- What did you learn from this activity:
  - about the Bible as a best-seller?
  - about how you think?

The Bible is a best-seller because...

...it tells great stories, about family, God, love, life and death – with excitement.

...it is the words of God, so people who read it hear God's voice for themselves.

...all Christians think they should own one, even if they don't read it.

...churches and schools buy hundreds of them to be kept in cupboards.

...it is the most given-away book ever. People give it to prisoners, hotels, babies, school children and anyone else who will accept it. This boosts the sales.

...it's a mystery book. It changes some people's lives, and gives messages of love, peace or faith to readers. People keep hoping to get the message.

THE WORLD'S NO.1 BEST SELLER

Responsibility pies: an RE Thinking Skills strategy

Activity 4: Bible metaphors

This is a sorting activity aimed at making sense of the place of the Bible in Christian life.

The following metaphors are some of the ways a Christian might describe the Bible. Ask pupils to match the correct endings to the sentence starters in the left-hand column.

For a Christian, the Bible might be like:

a **map** because…

...it can tell you what you're doing wrong, and help you do right.

a **comfort blanket** because…

...it can give people some hope for the future.

a **torch** on a dark night because…

...it can give you the strength to face the day.

a **fortune teller** because…

...it can challenge you to do your very best.

breakfast cereal because…

...it can show you the right path to choose.

a **soccer manager** because…

...it can make you feel safe when you're in danger.

a **police officer** because…

...it can light up the darker bits of your life.

Activity 4: Bible metaphors (continued)

Challenge pupils to create some Bible metaphors for themselves. These could be positive or negative. They should be written in the same format as those above. Examples could include: 'The Bible is like: meat / a probation officer / a steeple / a lion'.

These metaphors can be related to what Christians say about the Bible or God's word, for example as the bread of life, as a lamp to my feet, as a straight edge.

Activity 5: Bible cover designers

→ You work for the Global Bible Book Sellers, as creative designers. Your company is making a new range of Bibles for sale, and your job is to design the covers.

→ Look carefully at a range of Bible covers for some ideas, and design three in your group: one for children under 5, one for children your age, and one for grown-ups.

→ Show in your illustrations all you have learned about what makes the Bible such a popular book, seen as sacred for its wisdom by many people.

A guided story script: Enemies

I want you to begin by calming and slowing down your mind and being relaxed, so that you can let your imagination work. I'm going to tell you a story, in which you are a character. But first, would you get into a comfy position on your chair, and close your eyes, so that your 'mind's eye' can work. Spend a few moments getting calm: you can listen to the sound of your breath as it enters your lungs. Don't breathe any differently from usual, but just feel the air as it enters and leaves your body six or eight times. See how peaceful you can be (pause for around 45 seconds).

Now I want you to use your imagination. You are sitting in the school hall, on your own. It is a calm day, and the hall is cool and quiet. You hear the sound of someone approaching the door. Think of someone who you might say is an enemy of yours. Imagine that this person opens the door of the hall, and comes inside. Without saying anything, this person sits down in the hall as well. Picture yourself and this enemy: perhaps you are at opposite ends of the hall. Are you far apart, or close together? Anyway, you are both quiet — you begin by looking at each other in silence (pause) then after a few moments you ignore each other. In your mind, you are remembering why this person is your enemy. You are quite calm about it, but you are just going over the past in your mind (pause).

After a while, imagine that you look over and see the person you think is an enemy. They have their eyes closed, and they look as if they are doing the same thing as you. You try to imagine what they are thinking, what they are feeling, what they are remembering (pause).

In the hall, there is a loudspeaker which is used in assembly. Your eyes are shut, but you can hear that it is hissing very quietly, but it sounds just loud enough to make you think a tape is running. Some quiet music starts, and a soft voice on the tape reads out loud in the quiet hall: 'You have heard that it was said, love your neighbour, and hate your enemy. But I'm saying to you: "Love your enemy, and do good to those who hate you. Bless those who curse you. Pray for those who ill-treat you. You will then have a great reward, and you will be children of the most high God, who is good to the ungrateful, and the wicked."' The tape goes quiet, and the hiss of the player is the only sound (pause). Imagine that you think about the words: what do you think?

Imagine that the other person is just as quiet as you, thinking. You wonder what they think. In the end, imagine that you open your eyes, and look at the person you think is an enemy: are they looking at you? Is there a smile in their eyes? The other person says nothing, but there is a definite smile from them (pause).

Now before we finish this guided story, I want you to think about the story. It hasn't got an end, and different endings could be imagined. Perhaps the words would make a difference, and two enemies would become friends. Or perhaps not — maybe they would go their separate ways. Think about how this story might continue, and come to an end (pause).

Then, quietly, remember what the room was like before you closed your eyes. Remember where you sat, and what you saw. When you're ready, open your eyes again.

Activity 6: For 8–10-year-olds

Immediately after the guided story, ask pupils to work alone with a pencil and paper for 5–10 minutes to make a single image called 'enemy'. Teachers may want to use this time to talk to any pupils who need to talk about the guided story.

Follow this with a discussion: could the words of Jesus make a difference between enemies? Could this 'work' for anyone, or would it be more likely to make a difference between two Christians? How can enemies change their relationship — can an enemy become a friend?

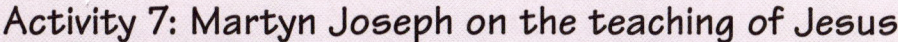

Activity 7: Martyn Joseph on the teaching of Jesus

In the song 'He never said…', Martyn (with Tom Robinson) contrasts the sayings of Jesus with some popular and proverbial 'wisdom' in a cut-and-thrust society like ours.

In this piece of work, pupils use the song as a stimulus to explore Jesus' teaching.

➔ Ask them to listen carefully, and to work out what Martyn is 'on about'.

➔ They can write their own poems based upon the same form – see the examples on the back cover.

He never said:

'God helps those who help themselves
Blessed are the rich
Do unto others before they do it unto you
Too bad buddy, the winner has to take it all.
Success is the key
You've gotta be cruel to be kind
It's a jungle out there
where the weak must get left behind
Archbishops should stick to theology
Put your faith in the lottery – all those little balls
By any means necessary
My country right or wrong
Send your money to me, touch the screen, you're gonna be healed
Every man's got a price, so do you want to make a deal?'

No. He said:

'Answer the stranger's cry for help
Love your brother as you love yourself
You only need to seek and you will find.
Forgive your enemy
Drop the grudge
Don't judge others and you won't be judged
Only knock and the door will open wide'

Lyrics © Martyn Joseph. You can buy Martyn Joseph's double CD Thunder and Rainbows (Pipe Records, 2000) from any good record store. It has this song and many more on it.

Things to note

QCA units into which some of these classroom ideas will fit well include:

3d: What is the Bible and why is it important for Christians?

6c: Why are sacred texts important?

See also....

- *The Miracle Maker* film and website: **www.themiraclemaker.org** (Bible Society/S4C)
- *The Lion Graphic Bible* (ISBN 0-7459-4598-8)
- *Teaching RE 5-11: Bible* (RE Today Services)
- *Belief File* video: **Pathways of Belief – Christianity** (BBC)
- **www.request.org.uk** – a useful Christian website.
- RMEP's series from the **Biblos** project *Everybody hurts sometimes, Meetings with mystery* and *Where are we going?* use an inspired and careful pedagogy to enable learning from the Bible.

Torah and tradition within Judaism

For the teacher

The Torah, the book that is the heart of the Jewish faith, is actually in its original form a scroll. Jews still read or chant from it every week in the synagogue.

Many Orthodox Jews believe that the Torah is literally the word of God. Liberal or Reform Jews believe that it is inspired by God but that humans wrote down the ideas and developed them.

As well as the Torah, Jews look to the prophets and writings in the rest of the Hebrew Bible for guidance. Tradition is also very important within Judaism. Within Orthodox Judaism in particular, beliefs and practices are passed from generation to generation through festivals, ceremonies and stories.

Most Agreed Syllabuses include Jewish holy books. Appropriate to the age and experience of pupils, learning should introduce pupils to Judaism and its significance for believers whilst making links to their own thoughts, feelings and experiences. These two dimensions – 'exploring' and 'responding' – are inextricably linked and RE should be a balance of both.

The activities which follow:

- introduce younger pupils to the importance of the Torah to Jews by linking the annual celebration of *Simchat Torah* with their own birthday celebrations;
- help pupils explore and express the meaning of *Shavuot*, the festival marking the giving of the Torah to Moses, through sensory experiences;
- encourage pupils to interpret and evaluate the importance of words from the Hebrew Bible for people today.

Fact file – Jewish holy books

Tenakh

- the holy scripture for Jews;
- it has three sections:
  - *Torah*, the five books of Moses;
  - *Nevi'im*, the prophets;
  - *Ketuvim*, the writings.
- the name *Tenakh* is derived from *Torah*, *Nevi'im* and *Ketuvim* (Te;Na;Kh);
- it is comprised of the same books as the Old Testament read by Christians, but should never be referred to as this.

Sefer Torah (Torah Scroll)

- is the most important part of the *Tenakh*;
- *Torah* means law, teaching or instruction, and comprises Genesis, Exodus, Leviticus, Numbers and Deuteronomy;
- it contains God's message to the people of Israel, providing laws and rules on which they should base their lives. It includes the 613 *mitzvot* (commandments) of the law, including the well-known ten commandments. These have become the basis for good behaviour in many parts of the world.
- the *Torah* began as an oral tradition, but was later written down by *sofers* (scribes).

Talmud

- the oral law for Jews, a tradition originally passed on by word of mouth, but now written down;
- it consists of the *Mishnah* and its commentary, the *Gemara*.

Birthday parties and the festival of Simchat Torah: lower primary

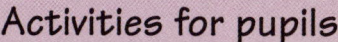

Fact file – Simchat Torah

Simchat Torah is the celebration of the reading of the *Torah*. It marks the ending and beginning of the annual cycle of *Torah* readings. Different *Torah* portions are read each week at Shabbat morning services.

It is a joyous celebration, involving dancing, singing, waving flags, eating sweets and parading the *Torah* scrolls around the synagogue seven times.

It is often said to be like a wedding. The people reading from the *Torah* are referred to as the bride or bridegroom of the *Torah*, reading the end of Deuteronomy and the beginning of Genesis. The wedding canopy is often held over the readers.

For the teacher

Simchat Torah is an annual joyous celebration. Look for a point of contact with pupils' own experience. A wedding ceremony would be ideal, but not all pupils will have experienced this. A birthday celebration is an alternative approach to help pupils 'get inside' what *Simchat Torah* is like for Jews.

Things to note

These activities link well with the following QCA RE Schemes of Work:

1d: Beliefs and practice (festival)

1e: How do Jewish people express their beliefs in practice? (*mezuzah* and Moses)

Activities for pupils

➜ What sorts of things do people do when they are happy? Show these using actions, gestures and movement.

➜ What sorts of things are worth 'celebrating' and why? Make a class list.

➜ Describe a birthday party or celebration you have been to. Make a class list of important words to do with how we celebrate – things such as friends, food, presents, dancing, games, fun, cards.

Listen to the story of Jonathan's Simchat Torah.

➜ In what ways is this like a birthday party? In what ways is it different? Make a list of similarities and differences. (Through probing questions, encourage pupils to pick out what is central to *Simchat Torah*.)

➜ Pupils could paint and cut out – or make – their own *Torah* scrolls and *Simchat Torah* flags. Use these to re-enact a *Simchat Torah* festival, reading a simple *Torah* passage, waving flags and dancing seven times around class. Pupils might sing and dance to the song, *Simchat Torah*, from 'Two Candles Burn' (see page 33).

➜ Make two class books of all pupils' work: one on 'Our Birthdays', illustrating traditions pupils have, and another on '*Simchat Torah*', illustrating how and why Jews celebrate *Simchat Torah*.

Expectations, based on the non-statutory QCA eight-level scale for RE

Pupils achieving at level 2 should be able to…

➜ say or act out what happens at *Simchat Torah*, and say why they think it is important to Jonathan;

➜ talk about a special celebration they have enjoyed, and say what sorts of things they think are worth celebrating and why.

Jonathan's Simchat Torah

Hello. My name is Jonathan, and I live in London. I am Jewish, and this weekend we celebrated a very special festival called Simchat Torah.

On Friday night we all went to the synagogue wearing our best new clothes. Lots of other Jews were there, and it was nice to be with everyone. For Jews this is a very special time of year. On this Friday we read the very last pages of the Torah – our very special book. It takes us all year to read it – and we always finish it on this special day.

Let me tell you what happens. We cover the Torah scroll in a beautiful velvet and silver cloth because it is so special to us, and we get all the other Torah scrolls out of the special cupboard where we keep them. Then we carry them round and round the synagogue in a sort of procession. Most of us children take our own mini Torah scrolls, so we all have something to carry. Then we sing and we dance and we go around the whole synagogue seven times. There's lots of noise. Everyone is happy and glad to say thank you to God for the Torah – his gift to us.

Many of the children

are given bright flags to wave. These are decorated with patterns and Jewish symbols. We wave them to show how special Simchat Torah festival is. My dad fixed an apple on the top of my flagpole, then he pushed a candle into the apple, and lit it. I had to be really careful when I danced with the candle on my flag. I do this every year so I am getting used to it now. My favourite bit of the whole thing is when we throw sweets at the people reading the Torah, and get some thrown back at us! These remind us that learning about the Torah should be a sweet experience.

The next morning – Saturday – we all go back to the synagogue. This time we read the very first bit of the Torah – you might have heard it – it tells the story of how God created the world. Sometimes we get a chance to read the Torah together, alongside the adults. One day I will be able to read the Torah by myself in synagogue.

I love the festival of Simchat Torah. It's a great time for us to have a special party to say thank you to God because he gave us the Torah. I love the Torah because it is full of stories about God, and it helps me to be a good person.

Celebrating the giving of the Torah – The festival of Shavuot

Fact file – Shavuot

- *Shavuot* celebrates the giving of the Torah to Moses on Mount Sinai (Exodus 19–20).
- *Shavuot* means 'weeks'. The festival comes seven weeks after Passover.
- At Passover the Israelites were freed from slavery. Seven weeks later they were given the laws they were to live by (*Torah*).
- In the Saturday morning synagogue service at *Shavuot*, the Ten Commandments and the book of Ruth are read.
- Some Jews spend the night before the festival in *Torah* study. Jews traditionally eat dairy products at this time. These remind them that the *Torah* is 'like milk and honey'.

For the teacher

This festival illustrates just how central the *Torah* is to Jews – it is the book of God's laws, given to them at Mount Sinai. By accepting and promising to live by these laws the Jews became God's people. Shavuot celebrates this new beginning.

Making and keeping promises is central here. The Jews promised to keep God's laws. In return God promised to make them into a great nation and to give them a land 'flowing with milk and honey' (the promised land). This agreement is known as the Covenant.

Using the senses to explore Shavuot

Pupils enjoy learning by using a variety of senses – sight, sound, touch, taste, smell. *Shavuot* provides a good opportunity for helping pupils use sight, sound and taste to interpret the meaning and significance of *Shavuot* for Jews today.

Activities for pupils

Sight

→ Arrange a display of dairy and honey products such as cheesecake, sweet Greek yoghurt flavoured with honey, honey-flavoured biscuits, or simply honey spread on fingers of bread.

Touch and taste

→ Encourage those who wish to taste some of these. This could be made into a game with pupils blindfolded and other pupils noting what they think each is and what it tastes like.

Tell

→ Tell pupils that Jews have a special festival called *Shavuot* at which it is usual to eat dairy dishes such as cheesecake. Tell them what happens at *Shavuot* and ask them why they think rich foods are appropriate at this time.

→ Tell pupils the *Torah* describes the land of Israel as a land flowing with milk and honey (Exodus 3:8), and Psalm 119:103 describes God's promises as sweeter than honey. For Jews, the *Torah* and the promised land are like milk and honey – talk about what this means.

→ Remind pupils of the story of Pooh Bear and how he loved honey. Discuss what is like milk and honey for pupils: What do they care about? What matters most for them? What is special in their lives? Pupils could produce posters to illustrate and explain their 'milk and honey', using creamy coloured sugar paper shaped like a traditional milk jug and yellow paper shaped like a pot of honey.

See also...

The **Jewish Children's Learning Network** website gives details of how *Shavuot* is celebrated:

www.akhlah.com/holidays/Shavuot

A better life: exploring some wise sayings from the Hebrew Bible
An activity for older primary pupils

The wise sayings below are guidance from the Hebrew Bible about how Jews can live lives as good as they believe God meant them to be.

→ Copy and enlarge the verses, making them into cards for pairs of pupils.

→ Ask pupils to sort the cards, putting the six which offer the best advice for Jews at the top.

→ For these six, pupils should explain what difference each would make if Jews followed the advice.

→ Pupils choose the two quotes they think are the best advice for everyone and work out a statement to support their point of view. They could also either draw a cartoon or role-play a situation showing what happens when the advice is not followed. Feed back ideas to the class.

→ In pairs, pupils improvise a telephone conversation between a Jewish aunt or uncle advising their niece or nephew as they begin their life at university. The aunt or uncle is keen to encourage the young person to remember God's guidance and to keep the traditions of Judaism. Pupils should refer to the wise saying quotations provided.

Respect your parents or those who care for you. *Exodus 20:12*	**Don't be jealous about what others have got.** *Exodus 20:17*
Be happy in obeying God's law and studying it day and night. *Psalm 1:2*	**Love and keep God's law. Remember it and think about it all day long.** *Psalm 119:97–98*
Put God first in your life. *Exodus 20:3*	**There is one God. Love God with all your heart, soul and strength.** *Deuteronomy 6:4–5*
Don't kill anyone. *Exodus 20:13*	**Be faithful to the person you marry.** *Exodus 20:14*
Love others as you love yourself. *Leviticus 19:18*	**Don't tell lies about people.** *Exodus 20:16*
Don't love anything more than you love God. *Exodus 20:4–5*	**Keep one day a week to rest and worship God.** *Exodus 20:8*
Keep your hands off what belongs to other people. *Exodus 20:15*	**Respect God's name.** *Exodus 20:7*

Wise words

For the teacher

In Judaism's Bible, there is a whole genre of wisdom literature, especially the books of Proverbs, Job and Ecclesiastes. In ancient Judaism, this literature was taught to young men in wisdom academies so that they would know how to cope with life. Many people today still look to these scriptures for advice and guidance.

The activity outlined here presents older primary pupils with some of these wise sayings and asks them to evaluate their 'wisdom' for today.

Activities for pupils

→ Copy and enlarge the following wise sayings from Proverbs chapter 15.

→ In pairs, pupils talk about what each means and decide which ones offer good advice for today. Feed back ideas to the class.

→ Each pair selects one proverb and works out a short role-play to show what the proverb means for today. These can be acted out to the class. Class members have to identify the proverb being acted out.

→ Class vote: 'Advice from the past can help us live better lives today'. Agree or disagree?

Wise sayings (Proverbs 15)

A gentle answer quietens anger, but a harsh one stirs up anger. *(verse 1)*

Kind words bring healing and life, but lying words make you feel crushed. *(verse 4)*

People who are big-headed and make fun of other people do not like to be corrected; they don't ask for help from wiser people. *(verse 12)*

It is better to eat a simple meal with people you love than to eat the finest meal where there is hate. *(verse 17)*

People who are bad-tempered cause arguments, but people who are patient calm people down. *(verse 18)*

If you are lazy you will have problems wherever you go, but if you are honest, you will have no trouble. *(verse 19)*

A smiling face makes you happy, and good news makes you feel better. *(verse 30)*

If you refuse to learn, you are hurting yourself. If you accept correction you will become wiser. *(verse 32)*

Things to note

The activities on pages 13, 14 and 15 link with the QCA RE schemes of work:

2a: What is the *Torah* and why is it important to Jewish people?

2c: Celebrations (focusing on a festival such as *Simchat Torah*)

6a: Worship and community

6c: Why are sacred texts important? (Generic)

Expectations, based on the non-statutory QCA eight-level scale for RE

Pupils working at level 4 should be able to:

• describe some things the Torah teaches about how people should behave towards one another;

• interpret the meanings of Jewish proverbs and apply these to everyday situations;

• express their own ideas and opinions about what is wise advice to follow.

The Qur'an – revelation, authority and influence

For the teacher

- Important as the **Prophet Muhammad** ﷺ is to **Muslims**, he is not important in himself but because he is regarded as the final and greatest prophet of **Allah**, the recipient of Allah's revelation recorded in the **Qur'an**.

- **Qur'an** means '**recitation**' and the **Arabic** words are meant for reading aloud wherever possible. Muslims believe the **Qur'an** to be the actual words of Allah received over a period of time by the Prophet Muhammad through the **Angel Jibril** (Gabriel). The festival of *Laylat-ul-Qadr* (the Night of Power or Majesty), celebrated on the 27th day of **Ramadan**, commemorates the revelation of this sacred book of **Islam**.

- Since it is believed that these are the actual words of Allah, it is important to keep the **Qur'an** in Arabic. It has been translated into other languages, but when translated it is not regarded as the proper **Qur'an**. For this reason Muslims all over the world learn Arabic in order to recite and understand the **Qur'an** as Allah intended. Many Muslims learn the whole of it by heart – when one does so, he or she is called *hafiz*.

- The **Qur'an** has 114 **surahs** (chapters) and over 6,000 verses. Apart from the opening surah its chapters tend to be organised so that the longest comes first and the shortest at the end.

- As the words of Allah the **Qur'an** has **authority** in all things, providing insight into the will of Allah for humankind. Its **influence** is wide-ranging. It is central to worship practices, regulates belief, life and behaviour, and provides a guide for decision-making for the community and the individual. The **Hadith** (statements about what Muhammad ﷺ said, did or approved of in particular situations) is looked to after the **Qur'an** to help Muslims in their decision-making.

Possible learning objectives

Learning about: the Qur'an. Pupils working at level 4 should be able to…

- explain the importance of the Qur'an for Muslims and give reasons why it is treated with great respect;
- explain how and why the Qur'an is used as a guide for daily living.

Learning from: the Qur'an. Pupils should be able to reflect on and express….

- thoughtful ideas about how texts and words influence them;
- the values and beliefs which influence their own lives;
- thoughtful responses about who or what is an authority in their own life – where do they turn for guidance or reassurance?

The activities outlined on the following pages develop aspects of each of these objectives but tend to focus particularly on the 'learning from' elements.

Things to note

Upper primary activities in this section link to the following QCA non-statutory schemes of work for RE:

Key Stage 2 Unit 6d: What is the Qur'an and why is it important to Muslims?

6c: Why are sacred texts important?

See also...

www.islam.org – links to Qur'anic recitations.

www.al-islam.org – various stories of the Prophet and Bilal's Bedtime Stories section.

Stop, Look, Listen: Water, Moon, Candle, Tree and Sword **video** – '**Moon**' (C4 learning) – a 15-minute general introduction to Islam for younger pupils, containing a useful short section on learning Arabic and the importance of the Qur'an.

For the teacher

- The stimulus sheet on page 18 can be used individually or in pairs by older primary pupils to read the story of how the Qur'an was received and to reflect on a Hadith (saying of Muhammad).

- Explain the importance of the revelation of the Qur'an to pupils. Muslims believe that the words of Allah were directly revealed to Muhammad through the angel. For Muslims, the Qur'an contains the words of Allah. This gives it the highest authority within the faith community. (Note: Muhammad himself could not read or write. He was the messenger and did not influence the words themselves.)

Introducing the Hadith: an experiential activity for upper primary pupils

'I am leaving you a trust. So long as you cling to it you can't go wrong. That is the rope God has extended from heaven to earth. That is the Qur'an.'

Try the following blindfold activity to prepare pupils for the reflective activity outlined on the stimulus sheet (page 18):

→ Set up an obstacle course in the school hall or on a grassed area outside. Large cardboard boxes are good for this purpose. Use mats inside the hall in case anyone falls.

→ Choose a pupil to negotiate the obstacle course blindfolded – others watch but should not give any guidance. After the pupil's attempt, he or she goes out of earshot.

→ Take a long rope and get pupils to mark a path through the obstacle course for the blindfolded pupil. Bring back the blindfolded pupil to have another go, this time allowing him or her to use the rope as a guide.

→ Discuss which attempt was easier and more successful, and why.

Introduce the Hadith

→ Explore with pupils how the rope might be a good metaphor for the Qur'an. Draw out from them how the Qur'an is a guide for Muslims which helps them know how to live.

→ Choose some appropriate Qur'anic texts, depending on your scheme of work and the age and abilities of your pupils. (Some examples are given here – others can be found on searchable Qur'an facilities on the internet.)

→ Use a spiral text activity (example on page 20) to aid thinking about and application of the text to daily life.

Some passages translated from the Qur'an

Creation

God it is that created the heavens and the earth and that which is between them in six days ... Such is the Knower, the Mighty, the Merciful, who made all things good.
(Qur'an 32:4–9)

Eat of the good things that have been provided for you, and be grateful to God.
(Qur'an 2:172)

The Qur'an

There has come to you light and a clear book from Allah. With it Allah guides him who will follow His pleasure into the ways of safety and bring them out of utter darkness into light by his will and guide them to the right path.
(Qur'an 5:15–16)

A code for living

Worship none but Allah; treat with kindness your parents and kindred, and orphans and those in need; speak fair to the people; be steadfast in prayer; and practise regular charity.
(Qur'an 40:83)

How did Muhammad ﷺ receive the Qur'an?

Often **Muhammad** ﷺ would go by himself into the mountains outside his home in **Makkah** to think about **Allah** and to pray. One favourite place he used to go to was the **Cave Hira,** on a mountain known as **Jabal al-Nur** (the Mountain of Light), about five kilometres from where he lived.

One night when he was 40 years old, he had a **vision** in which the **Angel Jibril** (or Gabriel) commanded him to **read** or **recite** (in Arabic the word is the same) some words from Allah. Muhammad protested that he could not since he was not able to either read or write himself. Nevertheless the Angel Jibril continued to command him and soon Muhammad realised that he must obey, and by Allah's will he was able to recite the words given. These first words received by Muhammad are now recorded in **surah** 96 of the **Qur'an**. The words speak of how God created human beings and how he teaches humankind 'by the Pen' (that is by the words of the Qur'an) what they do not know.

This was the first of many such **revelations** to **the Prophet** by the Angel Jibril. These now make up the holy book of **Islam**.

What is Laylat-ul-Qadr?

The '**Night of Power**' is an annual remembrance of the night on which Muhammad received the **first revelation of the Qur'an**. Many Muslims remember this event on the **27th of Ramadan** by spending the night at the mosque, reading from the Qur'an and praying. Some spend a full ten days in the mosque giving over their time to prayer, study and reading the Qur'an.

To think about

'I am leaving you a trust. So long as you cling to it you can't go wrong. That is the rope God has extended from heaven to earth. That is the Qur'an.' *(Hadith of Darimi 1)*

→ Think about the imagery contained in this Hadith (saying). In what ways might the Qur'an be like a rope extending from heaven to earth for Muslims?

→ Think about things (people, sayings and so on) that you 'cling to' and that give you strength. Draw a rope and attach to it drawings or writing about things, people and sayings that are important to you.

For the teacher: Spiral text activity

The activity on page 20 is aimed at upper primary pupils. It is a spiral text activity which provides a series of structured questions around a key quote to encourage pupils to think more deeply about its meaning.

Devising a spiral text activity

Step 1: Start with a stimulus quotation (from scripture, for example).

Step 2: In the first box, place a question which asks pupils to interpret what the quotation says and means.

Step 3: In the next two or three boxes, devise questions which 'unpack' an aspect of the quotation.

Step 4: Add a question for reflection which relates back to the quotation itself.

The approach can be differentiated by the number of boxes provided and by the depth of the probing questions set. Providing more boxes (with easier learning steps) can be better for some pupils.

The example given is for individual (written) work but this approach can also be used to provide a framework for paired discussion.

Activity for pupils: Calligrams

Islamic art is famed for its abstract and geometrical designs and intricacy. Words from the Qur'an often form the basis of such designs.

Pupils could write a **poem** in the form of a **calligram** (that is, when the formation of the letters or the font used represents an aspect of the poem's subject).

The poem could be based on a text from the Qur'an.

For example, the Qur'an as a light in the form of a candle or a light bulb (see quotation on page 17).

Alternatively they could take the idea of **kindness** and write a **concrete or shape poem** based on something someone has given them as a gesture of kindness.

For the teacher: Activities for lower primary pupils

→ Read or tell the story of how Muhammad received the Qur'an (page 18).

→ Use the activity sheet on page 21. These approaches link with literacy objectives for pupils aged four and five in England. The Hadith has been simplified for these younger pupils.

For the teacher: A mnemonic

When planning work on the Qur'an, remember:

R evelation
A uthority
I nspiration
N ow me (application)

For Muslims, the concepts of revelation, authority and inspiration are intimately bound up with their love for and application of the Qur'an in their daily lives.

For pupils to begin to understand the importance of the Qur'an, they need to address each aspect. In addition they need to consider what the Qur'an has to say to them, and be set tasks which enable them to draw meaning from their learning about Islam for themselves irrespective of their life stance – for example, *What or who inspires me?* This is the *now me* element of planning.

What do you think?

3 What do the words below mean?

Justice is: _____

_____

Kindness is: _____

_____

Giving is: _____

_____

4 Think about when someone has been kind to you.
Write down three 'feeling' words to describe how it made you feel.

_____

_____

_____

2 What does this say about how Muslims should try to live?

_____

_____

_____

_____

5 What do you think are some of the ways people cause harm in the world today? Write down two things and say why you think they are bad.

1 _____

_____

2 _____

_____

1 *God wants justice and kindness and giving to others, and forbids causing harm.*
He wants you to take notice.
(Qur'an 16:90)

6 **Think about:** How might the world be a better place if everyone 'took notice' of what Muslims believe to be these words from Allah in the Qur'an?

→ Read the quotation in bubble 1. Think carefully about it and move on to bubble 2 – try to answer the question as thoughtfully as you can. Work your way around each bubble and back to the beginning.

→ When you have completed your writing, talk with a partner about your answers. What have you said that is similar? What is different?

→ Next, on your own: Choose one of the 'feeling' words you wrote down and write an **acrostic poem** based on it.

The Qur'an – A special book for Muslims

Qur'an
Earth
Heaven
Trust
A
l
l
a
h
M
u
s
l
i
m
G
o
d

'The Qur'an
is like
a rope
God has
put from
heaven
to earth.
Trust in it,
cling to it
and
you can't
go wrong.'

This is the Q _ _ _ _ _.
It is the special book for Muslims.

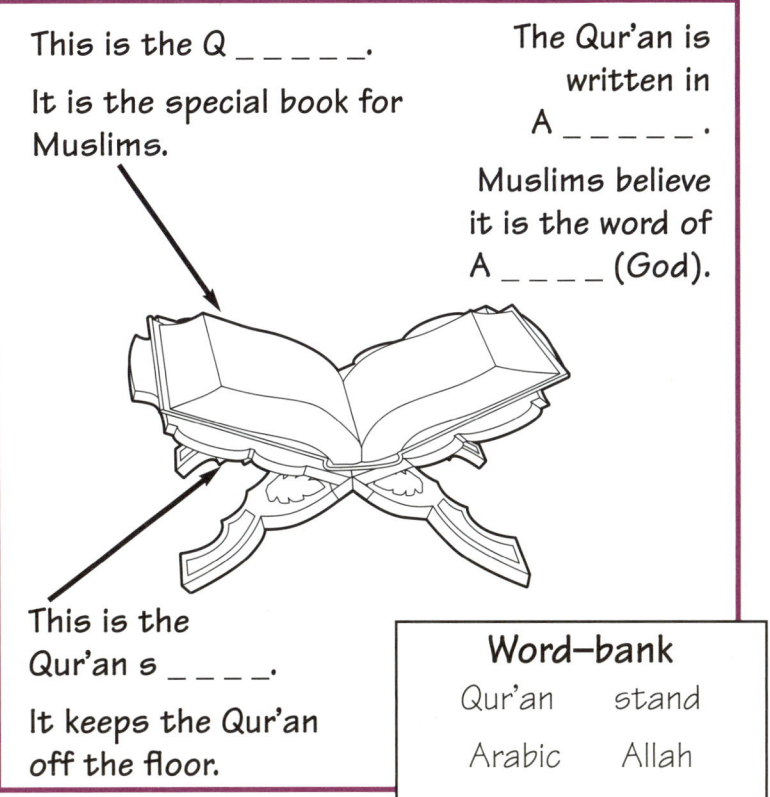

This is the Qur'an s _ _ _ _.
It keeps the Qur'an off the floor.

The Qur'an is written in A _ _ _ _ _.

Muslims believe it is the word of A _ _ _ _ (God).

Word–bank

Qur'an   stand

Arabic   Allah

Colour in **yellow** the shapes with **words** in them.

Colour in **red** the shapes with only a **letter** in them.

Using the letters, fill in this sentence:

_ _ _ _ _ is the _ _ _ _ _ _

name for _ _ _ .

Read these words with a partner.

Talk together about who or what you trust, and why.

Someone I trust is _ _ _ _ _ _ _ _.

I trust them because

_ _ _ _ _ _ _ _ _ _ _ _ _ _ _ _ _ _ _ _.

Learning about and learning from Hindu holy books

For the teacher: Hinduism

- Hinduism, or *Sanatan Dharma* as it is known by Hindus, teaches that all living beings are part of a Supreme Being (Brahman).

- Some people think Hindus worship many gods. The many gods are in fact different aspects of the one Supreme Being.
  'All gods lead to God as all rivers lead to the sea.'
  Bhagavad Gita

- Modern Hinduism places particular emphasis on three main gods: Brahma, the creator god; Vishnu, the god who looks after the world and keeps it going (preserver); and Shiva, the destroyer.

- Hinduism teaches that at times of moral decline Vishnu takes on human form to restore justice. Two of the more well-known *avatars* (incarnations) are Rama and Krishna.

- Many Hindus in Britain focus their worship on Vishnu, usually in the form of one of his avatars, particularly Krishna and Rama.

See also...

QCA unit 6c: Why are sacred texts important? and **unit 4a:** How and why do Hindus worship?

Developing Primary RE: Faith Stories (RE Today Services, 2003) – the story of Rama and Sita

ISKCON (International Society for Krishna Consciousness) – **www.iskcon.org.uk**

Vivekananda (Hinduism for schools) – **www.btinternet.com/~vivekananda**. Click on 'other links' for a range of stories from scriptures.

http://re-xs.ucsm.ac.uk/re/religion/ hinduism/writings.html for links to Hindu scripture websites.

Fact file – Hindu holy books

Vedas
- The main sacred writings of Hinduism, written in Sanskrit between 600 and 200 BCE;
- *Veda* means knowledge, which Hindus believe comes from God. These are *shruti* (revealed) scriptures.

Upanishads
- Means 'to sit down near' A sacred text based on the teaching of a guru (teacher) to a disciple. They explain the teachings of the *Vedas*.

Bhagavad Gita
- 'The song of the Lord'. Spoken by Krishna, this is the most important scripture for many Hindus. It is part of the *Mahabharata*.

Puranas
- A collection of remembered (*smriti*) stories about 1,000 years old. Many are about gods and goddesses and they include the stories of Krishna's childhood.

Ramayana and Mahabharata
- Two major epic stories of Hinduism.
- The *Mahabharata* was written around 900 BCE and deals with a power struggle between two royal families. The *Ramayana* is the Rama Sita epic told at Diwali.
- Many Hindus regard these as historical, not mythological, accounts.

VEDAS
UPANISHADS
BHAGAVAD GITA
PURANAS
RAMAYANA
MAHABHARATA

Activities for lower primary pupils: An approach to Hinduism using stories

For the teacher

Concepts central to Hinduism can be introduced to children from the early years onwards through the telling of stories from the faith tradition. Children can respond to the stories from 'where they are', and their questions are a key aspect of their own exploration.

Hindus can choose the way they wish to think of God. The important thing is to love God. Some like to think of him as Krishna. Some Hindus like to think of God as a little child. They believe that it is impossible for humans to look at God too closely – so God becomes a child, a brother, a friend, so that they can love him and not be frightened.

Stories of Krishna's childhood from the *Puranas* are a good focus for lower primary.

Expectations

It is important to be clear about what you want pupils to know, understand and be able to do by the end of the teaching activity. Below you will see three 'I can' statements which describe such outcomes in a pupil-friendly way. These are based on the QCA expectations for most seven-year-olds in RE, matched to the content of the teaching unit.

- I can tell you a story about Krishna.
- I can talk about some special words, symbols and stories and say what I think these mean for a believer.
- I can ask questions about difficult things and I know that these are the kinds of questions religions explore.

Krishna steals the butter

Sometimes young children get into trouble with Mum or Dad for being naughty. Can you remember getting into trouble? What had you done?

Lord Krishna was just the same. One story about him tells us how one day his mother churned some milk to make fresh butter. She kept it in a pot where she thought it would be safe. But Krishna found the pot, pulled it down and broke it! Putting his little hand in, he pulled out some butter and crawled to a dark corner to eat it. Just then a monkey wandered in (as they sometimes do in India), and Krishna fed some of the butter to the monkey. When his mother Yashoda realised what was happening, she told him off and took the butter from him.

She wanted to make sure she could keep an eye on him so she decided to fasten him to the table leg with a rope. She thought she had chosen a long enough piece of rope, but when she tried to fasten it she found it was far too short. So she got more rope, and still more, and tied them together, but Krishna seemed so big she could not get the rope around him! How could He, who has no beginning or end, and is everywhere in space, and who is all-powerful, ever be bound with ropes? Yet little Krishna, secretly smiling, finally allowed his mother to fasten the rope around him. Because of her great love, he couldn't go against her any longer and did as she wanted. She didn't leave him tied for very long. When she saw his cheeky face smiling up at her she undid the rope and gave him a great big hug!

Open your mouth

A long time ago, in a far-off land called India, lived a little boy called Krishna. Krishna had a brother called Balarama and they often played out in the forest. Usually they played well together – but sometimes their games turned to arguments, and sometimes they told tales on one another to their mother Yashoda.

One particular day Balarama burst into the house shouting 'Mother, mother, do you know what Krishna has been doing? He's been eating soil from the ground!'

'What have you been up to, Krishna?' asked Yashoda.

'Nothing,' replied Krishna, ' I haven't been doing anything.'

'Come here and let me look into your mouth' said Yashoda.

Krishna opened his mouth and Yashoda was amazed. She couldn't believe what she was seeing.

What do you think she saw?

There inside his mouth she could see all the stars and planets in the sky, the sun, the moon and earth itself, crawling with its many living creatures. She could even see the village and forest where they lived – as well as herself with Krishna on her knee.

Was she going mad? Was she dreaming? Yashoda felt very frightened. It was as if she was looking into the mouth of God.

Krishna closed his mouth and gave his mother a big hug. Yashoda knew that everything was all right. She knew that Krishna was her son and she loved him very much.

Hindus believe that Krishna was also God. Sometimes when people see God too closely, they are frightened. So Krishna becomes a little child, or a brother or a friend, so that they can know and love him without being frightened.

Activities for pupils

→ **Using pictures**. After telling the story, show children a picture from the story. Many are available in published packs or from the internet (type in a keyword and click on 'Images' on the Google search engine). Ask children *What can you see? Who can you see? What is happening in the picture?* Adults record key words and ideas.

→ **Questioning.** Ask children to each think of a question they would like to ask about the story. Take turns to ask. Talk about these as a class. Note down any that are hard to answer. Ask the children to pick out one thing in the story which seems strange or unusual. Talk about what this might tell us about Krishna.

→ **Use mime, movement or dance to retell the story.** It is traditional in Indian dance to tell the story of Krishna through mime and dance. Work out some hand movements and facial expressions for key moments. Make a tape recording of the story backed with Indian music. Join together in putting the movements to the story in traditional Indian style.

→ **Links to children's experience.** These are favourite stories for many Hindu children. Talk about why children like them. What is their favourite story? Why?

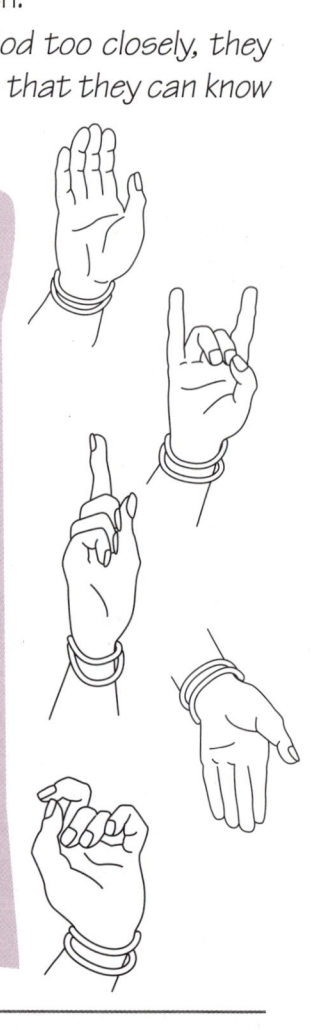

Activities for upper primary pupils: Arjuna faces a dilemma – advice from the Bhagavad Gita

For the teacher

Exploring dilemmas is a good approach with older primary pupils. It enables pupils to reflect on their own experience, apply the teachings of faith traditions and evaluate their own reasoned responses. It is particularly appropriate as an introduction to the Bhagavad Gita because the context of this epic story is of a dilemma.

The Bhagavad Gita is set on a battlefield. The Pandavas and the Kauravas are lined up against each other. In a lull in the fighting, one of the Pandava brothers, Arjuna, rides up and down between the opposing armies in his chariot. He has family on both sides – if he fights many will die; if he does not he fails to do his duty as a warrior. He is overcome with despair, realises he cannot fight and orders his charioteer to withdraw. The charioteer is really Krishna, and instead of doing as asked, starts a debate with Arjuna. The dialogue between them forms the Bhagavad Gita and encapsulates much of the teaching Hindus follow today.

The Bhagavad Gita teaches that you will only be satisfied with your life if you do your duty (*dharma*) without expecting anything in return. It is through unselfish action and devotion to God (*bhakti*) that people can escape the cycle of rebirth. Many Hindus read the Gita everyday for guidance, comfort and advice about life's problems.

Activities for pupils

→ Outline the story of the Bhagavad Gita to pupils and ask them to speculate about what Arjuna decided to do. (Influenced by Krishna's advice, Arjuna does his duty.)

→ Dilemma activity: Give pupils in pairs a set of dilemma cards (see page 26).
Pupils talk about:

- For each dilemma: What **might** you want to do? What **ought** you to do?
- What helps you decide what to do when faced with a dilemma? (Prompt cards may be useful here.)
- It can be hard to do the right thing. What kinds of things help us?

→ Feedback responses.

→ Explain to pupils that believers try to follow the example and teachings of religious leaders. Many Hindus are guided by the Bhagavad Gita, which contains the advice Krishna gave to Arjuna when he was faced with a difficult decision.

- Discuss the quotations from the Bhagavad Gita (Source 1).
- Ask pupils to decide what a Hindu young person would do in each situation if he or she followed the advice in the Gita.
- Class vote – 'Having a guide for living is really helpful.'

Things to note
This links well with PSHE/Citizenship Objectives 2f, 4a and 5g.

Dilemma cards: What would you want to do?
What do you think you *ought* to do?

You are given a large bar of chocolate. Your brother or sister loves chocolate.	You see someone you know stealing something.	You've been told that someone is saying nasty things about you behind your back.
You're invited to a stay over at a friend's house but Mum has arranged for you to visit Gran.	You haven't done your homework. Your friend offers you hers to copy.	You see someone your age throwing rubbish on the grass when there's a bin nearby.

Prompt cards: What helps you decide?

Can I get away with it?	What would my family want me to do?	Am I doing the best or kindest thing?
I always try to treat others as I would want to be treated.	If I did the wrong thing, I would worry about it afterwards.	What will my friends think?

Source 1: Words of wisdom from the Bhagavad Gita
(a Hindu holy book)

'Never try to avoid doing your duty.'

'Sometimes you need to give things up to help people and to please God.'

'Think of God when you work. Do everything to the best of your ability and not because you want a reward.'

'Any action carried out in love is pleasing to God.'

'Be peaceful to everyone, even people you don't like and those who are horrid to you.'

'If you would like to be like those in Heaven, be kind and gentle, find good things in people and forgive them, tell the truth and have lots of energy.'

'Love all living things the same amount.
Love a holy person or an animal as a friend.'

Sacred words of the Guru Granth Sahib

For the teacher

Video, discussion, group work, sorting, reflective writing, and application to modern contexts – these are the approaches used here to engage primary pupils with exploring the sacred text of the Sikhs and to get them thinking about how and why respect is shown, and what is meant by 'sacred'.

Activities 1, 3 and 4 are best suited to younger pupils, but all of the suggestions are flexible and can be adapted to both upper and lower primary.

Activities 1 and 2 enable pupils to explore the terms 'sacred' and 'special', drawing on their own knowledge and experiences and enabling them to identify what is sacred around them, within their own lives and within the Sikh home and gurdwara.

Activities 3 and 4 provide opportunities to reflect on 'what is worthy of respect' within their own lives and those of Sikhs.

Activities 5 and 6, aimed at upper primary, enable pupils to reflect on words from the Guru Granth Sahib and apply them to modern contexts.

See also...

'**Using ICT to study Sikhism** – a Year 2 activity' from *REtoday* autumn 2002 (page 32)

Sikhism: A Pictorial Guide (RE Today Services)

Teaching RE 5–11: Sikhism (RE Today Services)

www.sikhs.org/granth.htm

www.gurbani.org/kirtan.htm – to listen to recordings of *shabads* (hymns)

www.sikhkids.com

www.theresite.org.uk

Celebrating Festivals CD – features two Sikh hymns. Available from The Festival Shop.

Fact file – The Guru Granth Sahib

- The Guru Granth Sahib is unique among the world's great holy books because it:
  - is regarded by Sikhs as the head of their religion and the highest spiritual authority;
  - contains teachings from other faiths as well as its own religious leaders.

- The fifth leader of the Sikhs, Guru Arjan, began collecting teachings and writings into one book and its final form was given by the tenth leader, Guru Gobind Singh. He decreed that these writings were the ultimate authority of the Sikh faith and that there would be no more human Gurus. From this point it was called the Guru (teacher) Granth Sahib or Adi Granth.

- The book is regarded as a 'living' Guru because of the writings it contains, but it is not worshipped in itself.

- The Guru Granth Sahib is a collection of poetry and hymns, acknowledging God as the 'True Guru' and laying down guidelines for living, so developing spiritual salvation and unity with God.

- Every copy of the Guru Granth Sahib is exactly 1430 pages in length. Every copy has the same text on the corresponding page.

Activity for pupils 1: Sacred or special? (lower primary)

→ Display special objects that pupils have brought to school. Ask each child to say what their object is and why it is special to them.

→ Show pupils something of your own which has deep significance – perhaps a photograph reminding you of a special moment or a symbol of a relationship. Explore how these are different to other special things. Introduce the idea of some objects or symbols having deep meaning or significance and ask pupils to suggest other examples.

→ Slowly open up a box lined with tissue paper, and reveal a religious artefact. Talk about why this may be different from other special things – the care taken of it, the respect given to it, the importance placed upon it, the symbolism of it.

→ Introduce the term 'sacred'. Explain that lots of things can be called 'sacred' – for example, clothes, a book, a journey, food or a place – and use images from textbooks or downloaded from websites to illustrate these. Pupils could draw a picture of something which is sacred to a religious believer and say why it is sacred to them.

Activity for pupils 2: Sacred or special? (upper primary)

→ Do the words 'special' and 'sacred' mean the same? Or are they different?

→ Here are twenty words to talk about in your groups. You might need to use a dictionary to help you with some. Write three headings on a group recording sheet: '**Sacred**', '**Special**', '**Both**'.

→ Talk about each word, think of when or how you might use it, and decide whether the word best describes the meaning of 'sacred' or 'special', or if it applies to 'both'. Write the word in the appropriate column. You might be able to think of other words that could go on your recording sheet.

distinctive	respected	revered
appreciated	consecrated	hallowed
set apart	important	adored
loved	admired	blessed
religious	valued	spiritual
godly	holy	greatest
worthy	quality	

Talk about

→ What do all the words in the **Sacred** column have in common?

→ As a group, explain in no more than three sentences the difference between 'sacred' and 'special'.

→ Give examples of each of the following and for each pair say what is the difference between them:
sacred book/special book
sacred place/special place
sacred journey/special journey

→ Do you have special things and sacred things in your own life? What are these? What makes the difference?

Things to note: Expectations

Here are some 'I can' statements which describe such outcomes in a pupil-friendly way. They are based on the QCA expectations and matched to the content of the teaching unit.

Activity 1 (Lower primary): I can...

• talk about something which is special and, if appropriate, something which is sacred to me;

• pick out something which is sacred to a religious believer and say why it is sacred.

Activity 2 (Upper primary): I can...

• explain why some things are regarded as sacred;

• understand that people may have differing opinions on what is sacred.

Activity for pupils 3:
Imagine if someone very important came to your house...

This activity helps younger primary pupils practise ways of showing respect to someone. It uses mime, encourages speaking and listening, and fits well with personal, social and emotional learning goals.

→ In groups, ask pupils to imagine they are to invite a very special or important person to tea.

→ Adults working with groups could ask:
- Who would you invite? Why is this person very important?
- What would you do to get ready for this person's arrival?
- How would you greet the guest? What would you do and say?
- What would happen when they were in your house?

→ Provide pupils with a resource box of relevant items (for example, tablecloth, cups, plates, flowers and so on) and ask them to act out the scene. Follow up: talk about the ways in which the groups showed respect to their guests. Invite someone (the headteacher, a governor or the mayor) to the class for refreshments, so that pupils can experience showing respect for real.

→ Watch a video clip showing the Sikh holy book being welcomed into someone's home as an honoured guest and placed in a special room. Talk about why this is done.

Activity for pupils 4:
Showing respect

→ Talk about what 'showing respect' means and how respect can be shown in words and actions.

→ **Card activity:** In groups, give pupils cards illustrating objects and people which may be worthy of respect – such as those below. Pupils decide how each can be shown respect. This could be under the headings 'Things you could do' and 'Things you would not do'. Feed back ideas to the whole group.

→ **Watch a video clip** of the Sikh holy book being welcomed into a house as an honoured guest and placed in a special room or area of the house. Talk about why this is done. Questions to ask pupils could include: *What do you notice? What do people do? Which objects do you think are sacred to Sikhs? How do you know? What questions would you like to ask?* Discuss pupils' observations and ideas, encouraging them to mime some of the movements they notice. Follow this by watching the video clip again with the sound up.

→ **Mime role-play activity**: Provide pupils with a large book, some silky materials for wrapping the book, a table or raised platform with a large cushion, and a *chauri* (or something similar). Ask pupils to demonstrate how Sikhs show great respect towards their holy book. Follow up with activities to explore why it is treated like this.

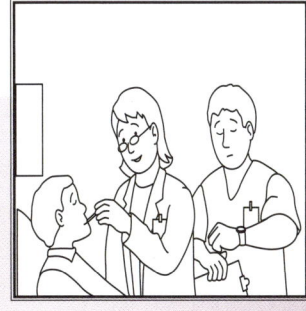

Hukamnama – sacred words of inspiration and guidance

Fact file – Hukamnama

- daily words of wisdom taken from the Guru Granth Sahib to provide guidance and inspiration to Sikhs.

- chosen by randomly opening the Guru Granth Sahib to any page; the *shabad* (hymn) on that page becomes the *Hukam* (chosen daily reading) for the day.

You can listen to a daily Hukam by visiting
www.sikhs.org/hukam_listen.htm

For the teacher

Activities 5 and 6 are aimed at getting older primary pupils to think about some wise words from the Guru Granth Sahib, to reflect on their meaning and to apply them to modern situations. The quotes have been simplified for use with pupils. The page numbers at the end of each text refer to the pages in the Guru Granth Sahib. You can find a full English translation via **www.sikhs.org**

Quotes 1–5 are easier to understand and could be used with lower primary pupils with a little adaptation to the suggestions for Activity 5.

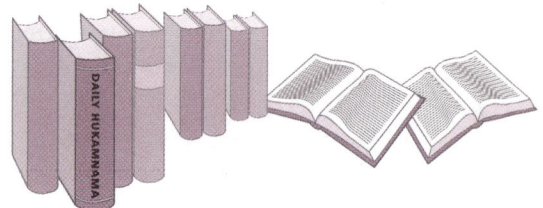

Activity for pupils 5: Daily words of wisdom

➔ Copy and cut up the quotations on page 31.

➔ In pairs, give pupils one quotation. Give the more challenging quotes (cards 6–10) to more able pupils.

➔ Agenda for discussion:
- What is being said? What does it mean?
- Do you agree with the advice offered? Has anyone offered you similar advice?
- Can you think of an occasion when you have used this advice?
- Feed back to the whole class. Decide together which quotation offers the best advice to them.

➔ Explain Hukamnama to pupils and that the texts they have used are sacred words from the Guru Granth Sahib. Listen to the daily Hukam by visiting the website above.

➔ Pupils look again at the quotation they were given. Ask them to decide what sorts of things their quotation might encourage a Sikh to do if that text was the Hukamnama for the day.

You could have your own *Hukamnama* for the day. Make a class booklet with each page showing one important value (be kind, be polite, be helpful) or one statement from the school code of conduct. Each morning a pupil opens the book at random, and the words written on the page become the focus for the day.

Things to note: Expectations

It is important to be clear about what you want pupils to know, understand and be able to do by the end of the teaching activity. Below, you will see four 'I can...' statements which describe such outcomes in a pupil-friendly way. These are based on the QCA expectations for most eleven-year-olds in RE, matched to the content of the teaching unit.

- *I can explain the meaning of some teachings from the Guru Granth Sahib;*

- *I can suggest how these teachings might make a difference to a Sikh;*

- *I can use the guidance offered in the Guru Granth Sahib and apply it to situations today;*

- *I can offer my own thoughts and ideas about some of these sacred texts.*

Wise words from the Guru Granth Sahib

1 If you tell lies, they will be found out;
the truth always comes out in the end.

(page 953)

6 Where there is forgiveness,
there is God himself.

(page 1372)

2 The best thing you can do is
to try to always help others.

(page 992)

7 Whoever realises what God wants and does
it, shall get to know God better.

(page 885)

3 Those who beat you with fists,
do not treat in the same manner,
but go to their house and kiss their feet.

(page 1378)

8 God is always with you –
never think that He is far away, and through
the Master's teaching, recognise God in yourself.

(page 116)

4 You should not argue with your parents,
but respect them. After all, it is thanks to them
that you have grown to be the age you are.

(page 1200)

9 Deep within you is the Light of God. It
radiates through everything he has made.
Through the master's teachings everlasting
peace is found.

(page 126)

5 God will judge and punish bullies
and look after those who try to follow Him.

(page 199)

10 There are those who read the Vedas and others –
Christians, Jews, Muslims – who read the Semitic
scriptures ... Guru Nanak says that whoever realises
the will of the Lord, He will find out the Lord's secrets!

(page 885)

Activity for pupils 6

Have you ever seen 'problem page' letters in magazines, those in which someone writes asking for help and advice? Imagine the letters below were written by young Sikhs, about your age. If you were a Sikh 'Agony Aunt', how would you use the sacred words of guidance from the Guru Granth Sahib to reply to the following letters?

Dear Agie

I was really fed up with my friend the other day. I went to her house for tea, which was OK but she started arguing with her mum, saying she was fussing and embarrassing her. Then she seemed to get angry and shouted at her mum and told her she was stupid. Her mum looked so sad, and I felt really embarrassed, but she just went quiet and went out of the room. My friend laughed and said that at last we could have a bit of privacy. But I was really surprised and said she shouldn't have shouted at her mum. She said she was always arguing with her mum and she went all moody and told me to go home.

Dear Agie

Me and my friends were in town the other day looking at some new Xbox games. While some of us were playing on the games consoles in the shop I heard two of my friends, Dan and Mark, talking. Dan was telling Mark to stuff one of the games down his trousers, and called him chicken when he refused. Mark went bright red, stuffed the game down his trousers and ran out of the shop, with Dan following. The others hadn't noticed anything was going on until the door theft alarms went off. The shop assistant was furious and asked us who the boys were. We all said we didn't know but they didn't believe us. I'm worried because the shop manager said they are going to contact our school and the police. What should I do?

Try this ...
some further activities

Engaging with characters and teachings in sacred texts

Guess who?

→ The teacher 'becomes' a key character from the text – perhaps David in the story of David and Goliath or Jairus in the miracle story or Arjuna in the Bhagavad Gita. (Remember that there are sensitivities about representing Muhammad or other prophets in Islam).

→ The class is divided into three teams. In turn each team asks questions to which the teacher can only answer 'yes' or 'no'. A team can guess who the character is when it is their turn. Be careful – correct guesses mean 6 points but incorrect ones give 2 points to each of the other teams.

→ This is useful as a summary activity after exploring stories and events in holy books.

Freeze-framing a key moment

→ In groups, pupils identify a key moment or turning point in a sacred story.

→ Each group role-plays the moment, freezing the action at the key point. A digital photograph is taken.

→ Using a word processing package, 'draw' thought bubbles from each character; pupils (in role) type in what their character is thinking. Give each pupil a copy with an extra thought bubble with the tail pointing off the page. Individually, pupils write in their own response to the story focusing on what it makes them think about or consider.

→ Note: See 'Stilling of the storm' activity with younger pupils in National Curriculum online (**www.nc.uk.net**), RE exemplification section.

Considering some key ideas

Authority: Acrostic poems

Muslims believe that the Qur'an has authority to direct how a Muslim should live because it is the word of Allah. Ask pupils to talk about who or what has authority over them and why. Pupils could then use each letter of the word AUTHORITY to make an acrostic to express their thoughts.

Inspiration: Jigsaw texts

Many people believe that their scriptures are 'inspired' and that they offer inspiration to believers. Select, type up in a large font and copy onto card short texts from the scripture(s). Cut these into jigsaw-type pieces. Pupils piece together the jigsaw and talk about the kind of behaviour the text might inspire. They could then choose a piece of writing which they find 'inspiring' and share this with their group or class, saying why.

God: They believe/I believe

Provide up to eight statements from the scripture(s) under consideration that say something about God. In pairs, pupils compare and contrast these and then each writes their own statement about what they believe about God or questions they would like to ask God.